A Beer with The Devil

By Darryl Harrison

I0455791

Pants Down Edition, License Notes

Table Of Contents

A Sizzling Performance

A Bizarre Bus Ride

The Sick World of Mr. James Beats

Free Draft Beer at The Corner Bar

The Very Best Air Racer

The Scandalous Birds

About the author

A Sizzling Performance

Dog, I'd been drinking all night, and so I felt exhausted and horrible in the morning. I still managed to get my butt out to work. I had been busing tables in The Cabaret Coffee Shop, in the Reno Casino. With the economy so screwed-up, I went through hell to get this crummy job.

The day got weird once a lady with a brown-sugar face sat in my station---seven. She'd a blond wig that sat on her head crooked. She appeared to be an old cabaret girl from back-in-the-day. She'd massive sagging breast. She dressed in a cheap outfit. She smelled just like bug spray. I said hello and poured her some coffee. She blew-out a loud fart. Every one of the faces in the coffee shop squinted and many moved away.

"Keep the coffee coming child. Yo, young-bruh, I'm waiting for a friend. You dig?" she explained strongly, smacking me on the ass.

"Okay, fine," I said strongly with a forced smile.

Her breath smelled worst than her farts.

I poured her several cups of coffee once her guest finally showed-up. He had been a little man with alabaster skin, wearing a huge black jacket. He wanted coffee too. He looked kinda smart. I sat and watched them. She let off several more stink bombs.

"I'm Tomeka, baby," she stated strongly with a laugh and farted.

"I'm Steve Levy," he stated strongly with a smile.

"Nice to finally meet you," she said firmly with a smile and took a sip of coffee.

"You are so beautiful," he said sharply with a huge grin and slurped his coffee loudly. "Just like I imagined."

"I know, baby!" she boasted sharply, drinking her coffee down.

"This place isn't too bad," he said firmly looking it over with a grin.

"You know Bill Cosby ate in here? He told jokes on stage. During that time, this joint had class. You dig?" she explained strongly and farted.

We'd a good piano player on stage, playing something from Busoni.

"It was," he said firmly with a smile and continued to slurp his coffee loudly.

My waitress Kamilla had a face just like a pig and personality as big as her booty which was hella a wide load. She brought Tomeka an uncooked steak with lizard's blood poured over it like a sauce and grilled onions. I'd to run right down to a liquor store to get a couple of forty-ounce bottles of Olde English for the ratty old lady because the bar didn't serve the stuff. You feel me?

She'd a side of sweet potatoes and nasty looking fries. Levy had a hamburger that looked bigger than him and fries. He drank from a long neck Budweiser didn't fancy malt liquor.

"Hey, brother, I need those tables cleaned," the hostess stated harshly to me.

Levy and Tomeka ate, drank heavily and chatted about our chicken neck waitress in station five. They chuckled out loudly, annoying many customers. They ran Kamilla about just like a clown ignorant-fool getting side orders of this and that...more ketchup, butter, etc.

I took my thirty-five minute lunch break, eating a huge cheeseburger. I went along to the bathroom and threw-up and returned to work. Levy and Tomeka had been eating pie.

"Every time I stroll over there it smells just like a gas leak. That man will need to go sit on the toilet," Kamilla said harshly to me.

"Dog, it's not the dude. It's the old broad," I stated strongly.

The piano player had taken his break.

Tomeka took out a small radio from her raggedy purse and turned up some hella loud rap music. It had been so loud heads turned. She kept farting the whole time. Nobody wanted to sit near their table.

"Kiss it, baby," she said strongly to Levy.

"Yeh," he said sharply with a laugh.

"Do you dance, Mr. Levy?" she asked strongly with a smile.

"Well, you know what they say about white boys?" he said sharply with a laugh.

"Come on, boo! I'll guide you," she stated strongly, grabbing him up by the arm all most pulling it off.

Levy, Tomeka swayed back, and forth side-to-side to the music. Irritated faces had been watching. He was shorter. His face had been buried in her ugly breast. He kept stepping on her toes. They danced about recklessly knocking over chairs and bumping tables. The customers complained---some left. Next, she started doing the funky chicken. At one point, I thought the old broad was going keel over dead. After that, they started dancing close. She kissed him, shoving her tongue down his throat. He pulled back swiftly, eyes narrowed with disgust.

"Baby, don't do that again. Dude, I nearly choked. It felt just like a snake went down my throat. Sister, your breath has the scent of beer and frog-poop," he stated haughtily with a frown.

"Well, Billy De Williams never complained," she said sharply and farted. "Kiss it, baby."

"Yeah, mama!" he said firmly with a smile.

Levy dipped her down almost falling over and she farted loudly. All the folks in the coffee shop eyes narrowed with disgust. He brought her back up.

"Kiss it baby," she said strongly with a laugh.

"Yeah, mama," he said happily.

After ten more loud rap songs, they finally sat back down.

"They must be on drugs," Karmilla said maliciously, looking shocked.

"Bruh, I wonder why security hasn't tossed this old lady and her slimy friend out by now," I stated hotly, shaking my head

"You're great, Tomeaka," Levy stated firmly with a laugh.

"Child, you got your dance-on too," she stated.

"Hey, Miss, why don't you and that four-eyed frog-brain get me and my partner some whiskey," Tomeka ordered sharply, farting.

The cocktail waitress delivered the mouthy old broad her drinks. I met Miya, a busgirl doing work in the seafood restaurant, in the bathroom exactly where she made love with me in front a Philipino man who had been cleaning the stink hole. Afterwards we smoked a huge joint. Next, I hurried back to the kitchen where my Mexican dishwasher buddy had my clean silverware.

A blond Russian-looking hostess was screaming at me because she needed those three tables cleaned. Dog, I bused them as I observed

Levy and Tomeka. The piano player returned, playing classical stuff by Liszt. I believe it had been Etudes d' execution transcend ante.

"Bro-bro, I had been here when Jackie Robinson hit those home runs that won the series. You ought to have witnessed how packed this joint was," Tomeka explained sharply with a laugh and farted.

"No way! Blacks weren't allowed in here in '47," Levy explained firmly with a smirk, shaking his head.

"Bruh, I'm a showgirl. You dig? Baby, I performed here---on that very stage. Dog, I sung My Jackie Come To Town To Win The World Series," she said strongly and lit a joint.

"Dude, I don't remember," he snapped and took a long swig of his whiskey. "Dude, I mean I don't remember the song."

"You was probably too young," she snapped and took a long drag from her joint as she farted. "Kiss it, baby!"

"I'm not ready for a gay Mayor," Levy said brazenly with a frown.

"Child, the Mayor isn't gay," she said firmly, blowing smoke in his face.

"Dude, he sure looks it," he said gruffly.

"Loosen up, bro-bro. This is the nineties not fifties. You dig?" she stated sharply and slurped her whiskey loudly. "It's fine to be gay. Stop hating baby. I got gay friends too."

Tomeka put lipstick on from a tacky makeup kit. The red was smeared on her gigantic lips just like some six-year-old put it there.

"How do I look?" she said strongly with a laugh.

"Wonderful!" Levy said sharply, finishing his fifth whiskey.

"You still don't believe I'm a performer?" she said calmly and took a long hit from her joint.

"No. I think you're a crazy old lady. You're pissed-off due to the fact life has passed you by," he explained firmly and took a long drag to finish off the weed.

"Let me proof it, child," she stated strongly, taking out a lighter from her purse.

Tomeka lit the lighter. The flame had been hella huge. She lowered the flame down to the bottom of her cheap dress. She lit the edges. The orange and red flames moved up around her dress quickly---dry material will do this stuff all the time. Levy backed away from her with fear growing on his face.

"Tomeka, are you crazy?" he snapped sharply as he quickly removing his jacket.

"No honey! This is entertainment, dog," she stated strongly with a laugh.

Levy attempted to throw his coat on her burning body. She shoved it off. Following the flames began to consume her entire body. You could smell burning flesh. She didn't scream. She seemed hella invincible. She moved swiftly down the aisle like a flaming goddess. When she farted, flames blew out her booty like a rocket. The folks in the Cabaret Coffee shop had been in shock.

This crazy woman ran for the piano. The piano player quickly leaped up and ran off like he saw a monster. She burned, burned, and still didn't even scream. She sat down at the piano, burning away. She started to play...what sounded just like Until You Come Back To Me (That's What I'm Gonna Do). She had been blazing away just like some ghost rider demon.

She appeared to be a skeleton on fire. She didn't appear to have any eyes or face. She kept farting and flames blew out her booty like a dragon's mouth. She sung every note and played every key to perfection. The audience stared in fear. This scene had been off-the-chain. The microphone had been on fire yet it didn't stop functioning. The area started to smell of burnt flesh and wood. Security was standing there with huge buckets of water, ready to throw. But Tomeka started looking demonic and security got too afraid to throw the water.

Once the sizzling performance had been over everybody clapped and cheered loudly. Tomeka stood up and bowed. Security hurried over and threw huge buckets of water on her until the flames were out. The paramedics showed up and had taken this crazy lady away and Mr. Levy followed with an astonished look on his face.

Tomeka had been a tough old broad. She dealt with 5th degree burns of her entire body. She looked even worse than Freddy Krueger. The doctors didn't expect her to live.

The very next day her skin grew back to normal and she wandered out of the hospital, looking much better than she ever looked--- twenty-five years younger. Once news got out some circus promoters asked her if she'd like to join them and perform this amazing trick.

"Possibly if your moneys good," she said sharply with a laugh.

A Bizarre Bus Ride

I'm Darryl Johnson. I'm thirteen. I'm a scrawny little turd-breath. Man, I'd to visit my Aunt Patricia Berg's house. I detested it. I pleaded with my mom Gwen to let me stay at home. She just ignored me. My aunt wore a full beard. She'd breathe more severe than the smell of a sewage plant. As a matter of fact I could smell her breath at my house right now. Her house smelled just like a thousand dogs farted in there. She forced me to eat this atrocious gumbo which she had put some of her doo-doo in and her dogs and cats too. I'd rather eat paint. I adored the fart games we'd play. She loved to sit down on my head in the nude and fart all day long. She put her cigarettes out on my back all day long. Then put lemon juice over the wounds.

Dog, I continued to wait at the bus stop with five child molesters, and they forced me to smoking marijuana. Dog, It didn't rain today. The woman with a hairy bird face didn't come. Conversely, the real cool bruh Mel, who produced duck hunting sounds didn't either. And also where had been Mrs. Malarecki, that old bag? She'd pass by, bring up her dress in front of me, and if I didn't stick my finger into her rotten old pussy she wouldn't let me pass. Where were the streaking Rappers? Today was actually beginning to suck dog farts.

Next, the bus arrived and I got on. Bruh, I paid and made my way right down to the rear, where a woman stood there nude, yet a yellow leather coat covered her and a lot of her hot body to the waist. She'd very long hair, looked Spanish, maybe Puerto Rican. She came across as content and insightful. She had been reading a romance novel and smoking marijuana.

"Hello, miss," I stated strongly with a smile.

She didn't reply.

"Hello, Miss, hello, hello," I stated sharply.

She looked down from her book. Her face started to harden.

"Hi, kid," she said bluntly with a forced smile.

"My name is Darryl Johnson," I said, smiling.

"I'm Sheila Maiers," she said strongly.

"Miss Maiers, exactly where are your clothes?" I asked strongly.

"At home, kid," Miss Maiers snapped.

A black man with high Slavic cheekbones danced around the bus just like a ballerina wearing a dress.

"But aren't you actually cold?" I said clearly with a puzzle look.

"No kid! Dude, I'm sizzling. Isn't it hot on the bus?" she snapped and took a long drag from her joint

"Girl, it's not that hot, bruh," I said sharply.

Nobody on the bus cared about the nude woman. Everybody was doing outrages stuff.

"Stop looking at me!" Miss Maiers said coldly blowing smoke towards me.

"Dog, I'm sorry. It appears to be cool," I said strongly with a laugh.

"School is cool, baby," she snapped.

"Not my school. My math teacher made all of us students performs sex acts in front of her. Once we had been suitable, we'd receive A's. I believe I managed to get two of the girls in class pregnant. My reading teacher had been a child molester doing the nasty with all of us and nobody gave a damn. If we didn't let the poop-brain rape us we'd get a F. He got stoned and I had to watch him and a couple other teachers rape eight of my friends. The principle does Meth and listens to rap music and he's sixty. My English teacher made all of us spend the entire summer performing sexual acts with cattle on his farm. And we had to write a essay about it. My homeroom teacher makes all of us smoke crack cocaine, drank Coors beer and listen to heavy metal in the nude with a room full of live turkeys (birds). She claims its great therapy for us. And the school lunchroom served dead cat," I explained sharply.

"That's dreadful. This school ought to be investigated," she said brazenly.

"Hell, yeh! I don't want to go back," I said strongly with regret.

"You must find another school," she said sharply, finishing her weed.

"Yeah. I guess so," I said firmly.

She had large boobs.

"Can I feel your boobs?" I asked shyly.

"No!" she stated sharply with a laugh.

"Can I squeeze your booty?" I said firmly.

"No!" she snapped.

"Can I kiss you?" I said cheerfully.

"Sure kid," she said.

So she let me kiss her cheek.

"That was fun," I said.

"I'm sure it was," she said.

"Can I do the nasty with you?" I said strongly, beaming fondly.

"Maybe later," she snapped.

"I'm not a virgin. I was forced to have sex with my aunt and her dogs and cats," I said firmly with a smile.

"I see, kid," she said strongly.

The bus halted, folks got off, and folks got on. There had been some poor folks eating their doo-doo. A man had been drinking Olde English and making duck sounds. A Spanish dude had been passing a massive joint around. These black kids tossed about some Chinese girl's funky panties. She kept trying to get them back. The bus driver had been rapping, and sipping a can of Budweiser and sounded hella awful. A black man was selling crack cocaine to everyone who'd buy it. A homeless-looking white dude had been trying to sell Meth to passengers. A dwarf pissed and threw his poop at everyone on the bus. A blond woman appeared to be kissing loudly on a Japanese girl's pussy. A red head was soliciting free blowjobs around the bus but the lady looked so funky that nobody wanted nothing from her. Two white guys and a black kid were beaten up some nerdy fat kid. Some movie folks were filming two blond lesbians, with huge boobs make out with each other. The child molesters stared adoringly at me.

"Where are you heading, kid?" she asked softly.

"To my aunt's house," I stated clearly.

"Sounds great," she said strongly with a smirk.

"No! I'd rather kiss my best friend's pee-pees while he takes a dukey on my face all day," I stated bitterly.

"You shouldn't feel that way. At least you've got family. It's an advantage to have somebody who cares about you. I wish I did. I need that very much," she said strongly with sadness on her face.

The bus stopped and a guy got on. He wasn't wearing anything. He seemed just like a movie star. He made his way down the isle, and riders smacked his booty as he strolled past. He stopped in front of Miss Maiers. He stared adoringly into her eyes for some time. They began kissing like beast. She adored it. They proceeded to go at it just like animals at a zoo. He jammed his tongue down her throat and she choked. A fat face Chinese dude had his jeans down, beating-off. Nobody on the bus gave the impression to care.

"No, no. Quit it!" she said strongly when she noticed me still sitting there.

"What is it?" he said harshly, rolling his eyes.

"Dude, the kid," she said sharply with a sheepish grin.

He looked straight down at me as though I had been dog doo-doo on his carpet.

"Turn your face, dude. Shouldn't your butt be in school?" he stated bitterly.

"Damnit, kid. I was going to---" the Chinese dude stated gruffly.

"And so was I since that seems to be against the law around here!" the nude man said indignantly with a scorching look.

"It's definitely not proper, Mike," she said strongly with a frown.

"What's not proper, baby," he said harshly.

"We are here to express our freedom to be nude," she said.

"I'm sorry. Dude, I forgot. Your body is so beautiful. I couldn't help it," he said calmly.

"It's okay. I forgive you dear," she said.

"Dude, we need to establish a good example for our youngsters, dude," he explained firmly.

"Slime the kids!" the Chinese guy added moodily, pulling on a joint. "Let their moms and dads teach them."

"Okay, good. We'll go to your spot, dude. There will be more nudist so we can began our protest. You're welcome to join us too sir," he stated strongly, looking at the Chinese guy.

"Dude you made my year. You don't know how long I've waiting for this opportunity," the Chinese guy said strongly with a laugh.

The bus stopped at the corner of Sixth Street. Miss Maiers looked at me.

"Cherish the moments you've got with your family given that they could be your last," she said strongly with a smile.

"Sure," I stated sharply not meaning it.

They got off the bus. I watched them wander down the street with on clothes on as the bus took off.

Once I reached my aunts house, the cops, fire Dept., coroner and paramedics had been there. My cousin Janet had been there, too. She chased a stretcher crying frantically as two men guided it by. They jammed my aunt into the wagon as though she had been old laundry. Bruh, I was chuckling.

At least I won't have to eat that gumbo with her, horses and dogs doo-doo mixed in it anymore or even feel hot cigarettes burning into my back. And her pouring hot coffee over my head. Or poking my nuts with needles. Or have sex with her and her dogs. Or put my pee-pee on a block of ice all day just for asking for another piece of candy.

Dude, I celebrated her death by going to the store, stealing some candy and soda. Dog, I pushed over shelves filled with candy and potato chips.

"You little punk! Get out of my store," the Arab stated hotly.

"Slime you!" I stated boldly.

"You bad little frog-breath!" he shouted defensively.

This little booty-face chased me down the block. I ran through these kinds of condominiums, ditching the fool.

The Sick World Of Mr. James Beats

Mr. James Beats lost his job at the meat packing plant. He labored there for twenty years. Plenty of his pals lost their shit too. Our economy had been in the toilet. Beats dogmatic wife left him for his horse. His ugly youngsters went along to stay with a pal a child molester that ran a Meth lab in his garage. His sweetheart a nasty Meth whore couldn't endure having sex with him and his pet hogs any longer. His two-headed dog finally ran away. He had been about to lose his house.

Beats acquired an owlish face. He appeared to be forty-seven, maybe older. And ended up being uncertain how he could start over now. He had been unexpressive. He seemed to be oblivious. He smelled just like rotten hamburgers' all the time. He spent many weeks looking for a job. Yet finding employment had been as tight as a rat's booty. He rejected a position at the county circus that paid $18.00 an hour, because he had been too terrified to be locked in a cage with a gorilla whilst folks paid tickets to look at him being raped all day.

Beats traveled to his bank for a loan.

"You got collateral?" the poop-head loan-officer requested sharply.

"Man, you may have a sack of pig-farts. Or a silk gray suit with a hole in the crotch area," Mr. Beats stated sharply with a laugh.

"Hold on! Allow me to speak with my boss," he said strongly and hurried off.

Beats snapped up all of the chocolates and somebody's finger from a filthy bowl. He placed them in his coat. He couldn't hear the things they were speaking about due to the fact his back had been turned to them. Twenty minutes afterwards the bovine little bum showed up right in front of him.

"Dude, I'm sorry. My supervisor said no! Dude, your credit score is so-so. Yet you've no job and also your savings..."

"Okay, okay. Hey, man, I tell ya what. Dude, I'll kiss your feet," Beats stated strongly, grabbing at the man's crotch.

"No, I'm sorry," he stated firmly.

"I really don't want to kiss your feet. Man, I simply require this loan or I'll lose my house. Dude, I'll carry out anything. Okay, I'll lick your bosses' booty. Man, I'll kiss the woman with the lizard face," Mr. Beats said firmly.

"No! Will you go now?" the loan officer said strongly.

"Can I wash your car? Lick your dog's nuts! I'll wash your car. I'll do any lousy job you can think of. No matter how gross," Mr. Beats said sharply with a laugh.

"Get your crazy out of here! Security! Security, get this nut out of here!" the loan officer said spitefully.

Security dragged Beats across the marble floor, kicking and screaming.

"Slime you! Slime this sorry bank!" Beats said sourly.

Security tossed him into the garbage can. Everybody in the bank stared and chuckled.

Clearly, he appeared to be having a difficult time. For weeks, he ran throughout the house nude bouncing on the furnisher just like a chimpanzee. He produced sounds just like a beast and drew pictures with his dukey on the walls. He drank Budweiser; used Ether, Fly agaric and Lord knows what else. He stood on his porch masturbating in front of children walking to school. He smelled even worse than the usual pack of dead skunks. He often drank his dog's urine. He began eating his and his dogs poop. He waved about a Beretta Cougar .32 auto, threatening to kill himself or anybody who came near him.

Eventually he'd this idea, enjoying a German shepherd poop on his lawn. He looked into the best way he could make some dough to help keep his house. Pay a closet filled with bills. Get some good girls. Consequently, he placed an ad in the newspaper about eating anyone's poop for $200.00.

The ad ran for several weeks, yet nobody responded to it. This upset Mr. Beats and he began pouring Chivas Regal down his eyeballs and doing Crystal Meth and Fly-agaric to get high. He ran about the neighborhood nude, flashing a loaded gun and asking folks if he could eat their doo-doo for a new diet. He had been intending to end it. Then a knock on the door halted him from pulling the trigger.

A dude with a pinhead, wearing thick-rimmed glasses came in, he carried a large plastic bag and an awful odor came from it. The man's cheap suit had been wrinkled badly. He seemed mealy-mouthed. A genuine pig-brain.

"I'm Alejandro Mackey," he stated sharply in a drawling voice.

"I'm James..."

"Dude, I know exactly who you're," Mr. Mackey said firmly with a laugh.

"What's in the bag that smells delicious?" Mr. Beats asked sharply with a laugh.

"My doo-doo! Dude, you said in your ad you'd eat it," Mackey said firmly.

"You bring the fucking $200.00?" Mr. Beats snapped.

"Dude, I'm not going to pay you to eat my dukey," Mr. Mackey said hotly.

"Dude, just give me the poop," Mr. Beats screamed.

He took the very stinky bag from him and opened it. The stink hit his face just like a punch. His fish lips curled in repugnance.

"Dude, I can't believe anybody's crazy enough to eat my poop," Mr. Mackey said strongly with a puzzled look on his face. "Nobody will believe me."

Mr. Beats grabbed a handful of poop and shoved it into his mouth. Mr. Mackey filmed it with his camcorder. Beats chewed it like hamburger and even swallowed it without throwing up. Mackey couldn't watch any longer and threw up green slimy stuff on the floor.

"Dude you're so gross!" Mackey said sharply, frowning.

He took off without completing the filming. Beats ate everything. He drank it down with Coors beer. The room stunk just like a sewer.

Mr. Beats sure didn't discriminate. A large black woman came over with big bag of poop, from her entire family. He sat and ate all of it, and drank red wine. The dude didn't flinch the whole time or throw up. She looked on shaking her head greenly. She felt sorry for him and gave him $300.00. A Latin lady and her boyfriend came over with their poop and he ate that too, just a little spicy though. He washed that down with Corona beer. Two gay guys delivered liquid stool samples. He drank that through a straw. Asian's came by with their poop. Jewish folks came by with large amounts of their dukey to watch Beats eat it. Old folks came by. French folks brought their shit for him to eat. Folks from India came over. Ethiopian folks came over, Swiss, Germany, Iran, Tokyo, Cairo, Bombay, Rome, Baghdad, Dublin, Athens, Honolulu, Jerusalem, China, London, Los Angeles, San Francisco, Johannesburg, Washington DC, Oakland, Brussels, Denver, Australian, Serbian, Nigerian, and Russian folks. England folks delivered their poop for him to eat. He enjoyed his feces with lots of hot sauce, salt and pepper. He washed everything down with urine.

Mr. Beats went completely batty. All he did was use Crystal Meth, pour whiskey up his nose and used an assortment of pills as he ate folks doo-doo all day. Some folks paid him because they felt sorry for him. The money he got helped him a little bit. But he was still $15,000 in debt.

Beats met this exhibitionistic girl Barbara Marcroft with a puckish face, blue to medium purple eyes. She'd an enormous right boob and a four year old child's like hand growing out of her left breast. She labored at Dee's Coffee Shop. Mr. Beats just went in there to get the coffee, anything else and you'd die he always said. Really! Last year half of the town's people died from eating in that place. She'd come to his house and they'd fuck, used DMT and Crystal Meth, pouring bottles of Sailor Jerry all over their eyeballs and taking large amounts of pills, along with Jimsonweed, Hashish, Nembutal and Speed. She complained about the pungent scent and his awful doo-doo breath. Other then that everything was cool.

Mr. Beats had been doing so-so now. He had been making a ton of money, mostly donations, but not enough to send his children to college. He relocated in an apartment. He purchased a horrible old Chevy. He purchased cheap pearls for Miss Marcroft.

Lastly, that old poop-eating bum felt ill and went along to an Oakland hospital. Dr. Marc

Boang had a careworn face yet had been inquisitive. He smelled just like beer and pizza.

"I can't believe I'm speaking with a dude that eats poop," Dr. Boang stated strongly with astonishment.

"Man, I was high on drugs frog-breath!" Mr. Beats said hotly.

"You can't keep doing this. You must stop taking all these pills, drugs, alcohol and eating doo-doo. You might die," Dr. Boang said firmly.

"Dude, I can't help it. I'm sick. I need help. I can't stop! It's the drugs. I've been using a lot--- Crystal Meth, tar heroin and DMT you name it I've done it," Mr. Beats said firmly. "I'm so fucked up now; all I want to do is eat poop."

"You really are a crazy old cat. Human waste has lots of deadly diseases and most common is gastroenteritis," Dr. Boang said strongly, shaking his head.

"Man, I don't give a damn, Doc. Just give me some darn medication so I can get out of this rat hole," Mr. Beats said hotly.

"The media would like to speak with you. Are you feeling up to it?" Dr. Boang said firmly.

"Why not?" he snapped.

Dr. Boang walked out. Next, the News 2 entered. Folks spent a couple of hours questioning him about eating so much poop. Then they left. He had been hoping his girl would likely arrive, yet she didn't. Perhaps she didn't find out he had been here.

A buxom red head nurse entered to take blood pressure and a blood sample, fix up his bed, and change his bedpan. Once she leaned over him to straighten his pillow with her breast pressing up against him. She came back with food.

"What's this stuff?" he snapped loudly, regarding with a lofty expression.

"It's food! And it's healthy," she said firmly.

"Baby! I can't eat this stuff anymore," Mr. Beats said hotly, shoving it away.

"You will need your strength. We simply cannot serve salt," she said firmly.

"I eat feces broad!" Mr. Beats said harshly.

"Are nuts?" she snapped with an evil gaze.

"Lady! Just bring me your stool sample or somebody else's," Mr. Beats said stubbornly with scorching look.

Mr. Beats pasted the time away enjoying football. He wasn't pleased about tubes sticking in his body, or machines, beeping all the time.

The nurse returned with patient's stool samples on a large plate. She clamped her nose with her fingers. Her eyes narrowed with disgust. Mr. Beats believed the woman might belch any moment.

"Aw! You're so gross, sir," she said strongly with her nose wrinkled up in disgust.

"You'd eat poop too, if you lost the coolest job you ever had along with your home and family. And using too many different kinds of drugs mixed with alcohol messed up your butt mind like me," Mr. Beats said firmly, shoving mouthfuls into his mouth.

"Mr. Beats I really could lose my job," she said sharply, staring catatonically.

"Don't worry I'll take full accountability. At this moment leave me unless you desire to kiss me!" he stated hotly, chewing.

She frowned and stormed out. He gulped down more doo-doo, washing it down with water.

Next, the spontaneous man, having a chestnut complexion and a Mohawk entered. His clothes smelled just like marijuana.

"It smells like dukey in here," the man said bluntly with a big frown.

"I just had dinner, bruh," Mr. Beats said cheerfully, picking his teeth.

"That's why I don't eat hospital food," the man said sharply. "But it smells like rotten baby diapers!"

"What do you need, homey?" Mr. Beats asked calmly. "If you ain't got no dope or a job for me, I don't need you!"

"I'm Delmar Jackson. I'm supervisor at McCladdie Sewage Co," he said strongly with a laugh.

"So what?" Mr. Beats snapped, sneering.

"I have been aware of your issues. I wish to assist," Jackson said firmly.

"Are you offering me a job, baby?" Mr. Beats said strongly with interest.

"That's right, sir," Mr. Jackson said sharply with eyes sparkling.

"Are you planning to let me swim in diarrhea?" Mr. Beats asked sharply radiating with good cheer.

"Man, I'd just like you to work as assistant Supervisor," Mr. Jackson said calmly.

"Lot's of cash?" Mr. Beats said happily.

"Anything you desire," Mr. Jackson said, grinning.

"Can I eat the poop and get high all day long?" Mr. Beats asked strongly.

"Sure, however, not much eating while at work. The CEO may not be too cool with it. But you can get high all you want to," he said cheerfully. "This job only hires people who like to get stoned on the job. If you're caught on the job sober you'll be fired."

"I want to eat the sewage too! I'll accept the work only if I can do that. Who wants to work at a sewage plant and can't eat doo-doo?" Mr. Beats said firmly reeling with unfettered joy.

"Okay, I'll talk with the boss about you eating some of the sewage," Jackson said strongly with a laugh.

"Okay, I'll take the job!" Beats said strongly with laughter.

Free Draft Beer at The Corner Bar

Dog, I lost my busboy job as a result of drinking and smoking too much crack cocaine. I had been two weeks behind in rent. I'd just buried my mother a week before. The misanthropic landlord was planning to put all my stuff outdoors and burn it.

Dude, I spent many weeks looking for a job. Dog, I was rejected by each and every casino. Trimbur's Bistro owner had taken one look at my poor butt and spit in my face once I demanded a dishwasher application. The supermarkets weren't hiring either at least for maggots like me. The economy had been dreadful. The job market had been as snug as a cat's booty.

Dog, I needed to scrounge fifty bucks from my friend Melvin Hernandez. He'd a awful job busing dining tables at an appalling casino. Bruh, I ate the very best steak dinner in the city. I smoked the very best marijuana around, G.

Dog, I felt surprisingly low. So I went to see my girlfriend. I wanted some cheering up. Miss Lataya Jackson had been an old fat woman; yet made love just like a dream. She was the only broad in the neighborhood with three breast. She picked her nose and ate her scabs doing crystal Meth and Percodan on a regular basis. She opened up the door. I came in. She had some lousy brown dude on her sofa with no clothes on. He had been smoking a joint and drinking Olde English. She began complaining about a phone bill. I ran the her cellular phone up as a result of phone-sex. If she wasn't making love to every bird-poop in the city I wouldn't have done it. Bruh, I got fed up with her bull. She had been very drunk. She desired all of us to have sexual intercourse, so I did. Then we all used Crystal Meth and some Psilocybin and had strange sex again with her pet pigs.

Things had been looking up once I stumbled on this big sign. Free Draft beer at The Corner Bar. There had been a huge line coming from the place. Therefore, I was standing in line like a dumbass but I loved beer.

Three hours later on, I made it to the bar. The animated bartender delivered me beers like crazy. The spot smelled just like two million dog farts, along with weed and sweat. The bartender had been smoking a big joint. Bruh, I drink root-beer flavored beer, watermelon beer, cola beer, chocolate beer, apple cinnamon beer, lemon beer, milk beer, pizza beer, lemon lime beer, fruit juice beer, V8 beer, chicken flavor and vegetable beer and even cheeseburger beer. This man had every beer flavor known to man. A lady having a horse's booty sat alongside me. She drank a chocolate flavor beer. Her name had been Aleka Ariff. She'd small arms just like Tyrannosaurus. She'd a kind face yet a red obscene mouth. The beauty of her had been her friendly manner.

On stage would be a bad act. An ugly two-headed woman with a huge breast growing out of her stomach juggled rotten oranges with six arms. However, the man without arms played great jazz music using his big nose on the piano keys.

"So what's a good chick like you doing here," I inquired strongly with a laugh.

"The free draft beer, darling," she snapped with a smile.

"Of course," I said strongly, grinning. What else?"

"I love free stuff, clothes, shoes and beer," she snapped with a laugh.

"That's hella cool," I said slowly, feeling hella stoned.

"Dude, I'd make love to you, but you're too ugly and short," she stated firmly with a laugh.

"That's exactly what most ladies claim...or too dark," I stated sharply with a laugh.

Miss Ariff kept drinking and drinking maybe then I'd look more appealing to her. Soon I'd began to resemble Denzel, George, Brad, and Matthew all rolled into one. She finally pleaded with me to make love to her in the bathroom.

It's something special in this beer. It took us two or three hours to get in there. The stalls had been packed with sex-crazed fools. In one stall, two homos had been making love to each other madly. In the other stall, a man with a big green egghead had been raping a monkey. Two black lesbians had been eating one another with lots of hot sauce. We returned to the bar.

"Did you know that a man's screwing a monkey in your toilet?" I inquired bluntly.

"Yes. That's Joel, he's blind. Jenifer's his seeing eye monkey," the bartender replied cheerfully.

"Dude, you don't make love to your pet," I stated hotly, shaking me head greenly.

"Darryl, you do if you're legally married," he said strongly with a laugh. "Hey, brother, it's nothing new for rich folks to jump into bed with their pets and farm animals."

"Those folks ought to take their butts home or get a motel," I explained bluntly.

Dog, I began observing demonic-looking cattle flying around in the bar, spitting flames with large red wings. After that, everybody appeared to be vampires with strange red eyes drinking beer-blood from giant mugs and many started biting into everybody's necks. I noticed massive watermelons flying about with large purple wings and sung my favorite jazz songs. There was George Washington and Abraham

Lincoln sitting in the corner drinking beer and sharing a joint. Martin Luther King was there drinking Olde English with a fly-looking white chick, showing plenty of leg. There were giant ducks walking around with human faces, carrying AK-47s and a huge roach, wearing an Oakland A's uniform on stage telling bad jokes.

All of a sudden, Miss Ariff had been floating about on a giant alligator with large spider legs and flames blowing out of it's booty.

"What's happening to me?" I said hotly with a puzzle look.

"You getting a little intoxicated my pal," the bartender stated sharply with a laugh.

"What have you put in my drink, dude?" I asked hotly.

"Our beer is rather powerful here. And some people are able to communicate with their dead love ones. You can talk to God. You can hear insects talking and understand them. You can communicate with your animals. Also when drinking our beer deaf people can hear, and blind folks can see. Also we've had folks that have lived to be two hundred years old. A woman was cured of stage 5 breast cancer. And also suffer from strange visions. Don't be concerned it'll wear off and you will be ten times smarter," he stated strongly with a laugh.

"Don't let me find out you poisoned me, homeboy! Dog, I'll check you punk!" I stated gruffly.

Miss Ariff yanked me close and kissed me like crazy speed freak. She rubbed up against my penis. She rammed her tongue down my throat. I nearly choked. Her tongue tasted just like chocolate beer, spit, lizard guts and marinated cow-doo-doo. So we made love for a short while. The crowd had been raucous. It had been difficult to make love in this crowd. I was just too many folks in this place. Nobody cared. Many folks had been intoxicated. And even high on crackcocaine, weed, cocaine, Amyl nitrite and Bufotenine you name it.

"Yummy," Miss Ariff stated cheerfully.

"Hey, baby. Let's blow this ice-cream stand. Let's proceed to your pad," I stated contentedly.

"Hell no!" Miss Ariff barked hotly.

"So you're a love them and leave them woman?" I said hotly.

She didn't answer.

Miss Ariff started to ignore me, as the night grew old. She began speaking with a dude who had huge claw-like hands, stuttering like some chipmunk with a face like a fly and body like a dwarf and legs like a horse. They joked. After that, she left with the ugly bum.

One stage right now had been a yellow-looking black man telling horrible jokes while a strange looking woman with a face like a snake with animal hair on oneside, kissed and licked on his naked body. She had a big blue eyeball on her left butt cheek and a sea creatures-looking hand growing out of her back. Also there was the face of a dog growing out of her right shoulder. The man tried to make love to her but she was just too much for the dude.

She pushed the man down backward and he landed on his back. The massive audience cheered them on.

"Come on baby! Tell us some more jokes," she said strongly with a spooky laugh.

But the yellow-looking black man just laid there screaming. Then she got down on top of him and bit into his face, removing a large chunk of flesh. She began to chewing. He screamed for help but nobody did anything. The audience was enjoying every sick performance.

The broad seemed to be incredibly strong and he couldn't push her away as she kept coming for another bit.

This time she took a huge chunk from his neck, and blood just spurted out like facet onto the stage and crowd cheered loudly. The man's screams got dimmer and dimmer as he was surely dying.

At this time, she had eaten half of the man. She stuck part of his leg to the dog and it started eating away. She shoved part of the arm into her booty. The teeth in her butt crack began chewing onto the flesh. The crowd continued to cheer.

As soon as she finished there was nothing but bones on the stage and a lot of blood. She burped loudly.

"Ah! That was hella good," she said strongly with a wicked laugh as she bowed.

The crowd applauded loudly for twenty minutes and she stood there all bloody bowing and laughing wickedly. Then the curtain went down.

The whole thing was hella gross and I threw up.

I got into a debate with a Chinese dude over baseball. He had been extremely high I could tell from his eyes. He'd three black dudes with him.

"So you don't like baseball?" the Chinese guy said sharply.

"Not really," I answered strongly.

"What do you like?" the black man asked sharply.

"Hockey, boxing, football, wrestling and basketball and making love to girls," I said strongly.

"Those are usually brutal sports dude," the Chinese dude said firmly.

"Dog, we're living in a chaotic world, baby," I said sharply and I took a long swig from beer.

"Do you believe in God?" the Chinese dude asked strongly, studying critically.

"Not your God, bruh," I said sharply.

"An atheist bum," one of the black folks stated harshly.

I didn't answer.

"Did you hear about the dogs, monkeys, cats, panda bears, birds, ducks, owls, lions, horses, tigers, cheetahs, lizards, skunks, leopard, goats, elephants, panthers, chipmunks, foxes, pigs, hogs, deer's and snakes get burned up in an animal shelter?" the black man asked firmly.

"Yep. Dog, I read something about it," I said firmly, sipping my beer.

"Well?" the other black dude stated strongly.

"Well what?" I snapped sharply with a smirk.

"Do you care?" the black cat asked strongly.

"Homeboy, I flipped the page. Bruh, I'd my mind on something more important. Bruh, I believe it had been sex. Lord, I hadn't been laid in six years," I stated sharply with a laugh.

"Well, you ungrateful frog-breath," the Chinese dude stated hotly.

"I'm sorry, bruh. Man, I'm sorry it turned out hella dreadful," I said sharply with regret and took a long swig from my beer bottle.

"It's dreadful, dog. You're a pig-breath. Maybe you got hot, maybe masturbated while all those animals screamed as they burned alive in some shelter with no windows," one of the black guys said harshly.

"Dog, if I observed it I would've experienced bad dreams about this. Dude, yet it's different in the event you read about this stuff opposed to seeing it on the news," I stated firmly, shaking my head greenly, finishing off my beer.

"Yo, black man, I'll bet you hate America too," the other black guy said firmly, looking hella evil. "Blood, you detest your mother and pet. And, church and everything. You feel me?"

I didn't say anything I wandered away towards the other end of the bar and tried to order another beer.

"Don't let me see you outside, poop-brain! Bum...you hating little turd-breath! If I see you I'm likely to beat the ugly black off you," the Chinese dude yelled harshly in a strong accent.

"What a buttworm! You should check that dude," one lady shouted sharply, an animal supporter.

"That cat sounds like Louis Farrakhan," one black man said bluntly.

At daybreak, the bar emptied out. Man, I staggered down the street to get a taxi. Once I got to the door, the Indian dude had taken one look at me and the scared guy sped off. I had taken a long piss behind the building. Next, the

Chinese dude turned up with three black guys, dressed up just like rappers.

This Chinese dude struck me in the stomach and I threw-up in his face. Brown and purple stuff ran down his face onto his brand-new Utah Jazz jersey.

"Yuck! You scumbag," he stated brazenly, frowning as he looked down at his shirt.

The Chinese dude leaped at me and grabbed hold of my collar. And directed his fist in to my ugly face hard enough that the impact knocked me onto my butt.

Whilst I had been on the ground, they kicked and punched, until I passed out.

Once I came to a Chinese girl with kernel teeth and frazzled hair had been hovering over me. She'd a powerful scent of marijuana. She applied a cloth with alcohol to my big cut on my forehead. Burning alcohols what woke me.

"Am I in heaven?" I asked weakly with a smile.

"Hell no!" she snapped.

"Who are you?" I asked hotly.

"I'm Joan Ling. I came across you on the street. You appeared as if somebody messed your stuff up, brother. And So I brought you here," she stated strongly with a smile.

"Well, thanks," I stated strongly with a laugh, attempting to sit up as I felt a little dizzy. The entire spot had been embellished in Asian. Hella nice.

"How are you feeling?" she asked sharply.

"Like a fish on the desert," I said dryly with a weak smile.

"Do you generally pick-up weird dudes?" I asked.

"Only when they're cute," Miss Ling said strongly with a laugh.

Miss Ling yanked down my filthy jeans. And she began to rape me like some speed freak.

"What are you doing?" I asked strongly, studying acutely.

"Relax...What's your name?" she said calmly.

"Darryl Johnson," I said sharply.

"Nice name," she said.

On the dining room table as I spotted red, blue, black, purple, yellow, brown, gray, white and orange pills. Also there were a couple of bottles of Wild Turkey in the chair. This lady has to be high on something to want to make love to my ugly butt.

"You don't need to do this."

"Shut up, gee!"

After it was over I lay on the sofa winded and helpless.

"Got any cash, baby?" I inquired strongly with a smirk as I grabbed one of the whiskey bottles.

"How much?" she snapped.

"Whatever you are able to spare. My mother has got cancer," I explained strongly with regret as I removed the cap.

"Sure. Sorry your mom has got cancer," Miss Ling said sadly.

"A dude needs to lay his head down somewhere," I said calmly and took a long swig from the bottle.

"You can remain here," Miss Ling said firmly as she shove a bunch of pills in her mouth and washed them down with whiskey.

"I got you," I snapped with a smile and took another long swig from the bottle.

"Do you get high?" she asked strongly.

"Everyday," I said sharply with good cheer.

"Do you need work?" she asked as she took a long sip from the whiskey.

"Hell, yeh!" I said strongly as I took a long guzzle from the whiskey.

"The bar at the corner needs an Iceman," she said strongly.

"Iceman?" I snapped.

"Just fill up the bar with ice. Any fool can perform that stuff," she said sharply, shaking her head greenly.

"Baby, I'll accept it," I said with a smile.

Lastly, things had been looking up. I was getting hella sex. But I was loving it. Man, I went down to my room to get my stuff. This unsavory woman placed all my things in the hallway. A bunch of creeps that smelled just like rat piss had been going through my stuff.

Yet the weeks just got hella better for a change.

The Very Best Air Racer

Dog, I was feeling blue. Man, I wanted to go to the Air-Races. Johnathan Pryce had been my idol. He had been very cool. He was the quickest dude and greatest out there. Bruh, I heard that cat flew through a hallway of a busy high school leaving without injuring anybody or messing up property. Which this stuff was very hard to believe.

However, I had been messed up. I'd colon cancer---well, I thought I did. There's a tumor the size of a damn gorilla in my crapshoot. When I took a crap, it had been just like defecating a panda bear with spikes. Blood and some pink-purple liquid stuff that didn't look like doo-doo dropped into the toilet. It hurt worst than hammering nails into my nuts. Good thing I had to see the doctor today.

10:30a.m. I had been at Brook Bear Hospital. Bruh, I had a scheduled visit with Dr. Earl Griesel. Dr. Griesel had been a cancer specialist. He sold crack in his spare time, yet very tactful. Dog, I had been naked, lying down on my stomach, on a large gurney. Dr. Griesel looked over my booty. I farted loudly in his face. That was an accident of course.

"Oh, Lord! What exactly are you eating?" he asked sharply. His cheeks bloated suddenly, as if holding back vomit.

"I'm sorry, pimp! I didn't realize you had been back there," I stated strongly with regret.

"Dude, I ate a purple steak."

"No wonder," he stated bitterly.

"I'm sorry gee," I said sadly.

"Well, Dijon. We're likely to remove this horrible thing," Dr. Griesel said strongly.

"Yo, I can't wait, player. Bruh, I wish to see Johnathan Pryce. He could be the fastest air-racer and best on the planet," I said strongly with good cheer.

"Man, I like him too. In an F-16, he did fifty-five summersaults at 675 mph. However not any of this could be true," Griesel stated sharply with a frown. He took out a joint and lit it.

"It is true, dawg. Are you kidding? Man, I observed it myself...with my own two eyes. It had been the best, man," I stated strongly.

"Did you realize that frog-turd had been intoxicated too?" he snapped, blowing smoke in my face.

"Hell no! Mr. Pryce is the cleanest dude I know. He doesn't drink and chase woman," I stated firmly.

"Listen son. We always think the most of our heroes. But once we meet them..."

"Enough of this bull. What about the cancer?" I asked icily.

"Okay. I'm going to put you out. Next, cut this awful monster out. Don't worry we have a 37% success rate," he said firmly with a laugh.

Following the surgical procedure, I had been left in the operating room. My butthole had been sore. I had been famished. The room smelled like strong black man sweat, marijuana, dog farts and death. Dog, I lay down there waiting for this poop-breath Dr. Griesel to show. Yet he never did. Not even that ugly nurse. It got dark. There had been no TV. Just blue monitors. Those damn things beeped and beeped. Before too long, I got a headache. Next, I went to sleep.

The following morning a coffee-colored, hot lady, having a boney booty came in, eating a slice of piazza. She took my blood pressure, along with a blood sample. The door had been closed. I thought about raping her. After that, escape out the backdoor. I chose not to---too weak.

"So what's up, baby-girl?" I asked strongly with good cheer.

"You're fine," she said sharply.

"What happened to Dr. Griesel?" I asked strongly.

"What do you mean?" she snapped.

"That buttworm left me here all night," I stated bluntly.

"I guess he forgot. I saw him making love with some blond in his office," she said firmly.

"Left my half nude butt in this surgery room for some bimbo!" I stated moodily with a monstrous glare. "I hope her pussy was really good."

"I'm sure it wasn't intentional," she snapped.

"It's because I'm black," I said gruffly.

"The doctor's black too, isn't he?" she said strongly.

"Sometimes I wonder," I said strongly.

"Let me go get your registered nurse. She didn't realize you had been left in here overnight," she mentioned strongly.

"Not that ugly woman," I stated harshly.

"You'll be all right. She knows her stuff," she said strongly.

"Baby, don't go. Sit on my face for awhile," I said strongly. "You're hella fly."

She smiled and wandered out.

The medicines wore off. My butt hurt. I screamed. It seemed like for hours. I threw up all over the place.

Three hours later on a brawny Philipino woman came in. She was drinking a Corona. She'd a horrible face.

"Where have you been? Didn't you hear me screaming? I screamed my damn lungs out!" I said venomously with my eyes seething.

"I'm sorry, sir. I was busy making love to a nurse," she stated strongly with regret, grabbing my bed and directed it towards the door.

"It's because I'm black," I said hotly.

"Don't say that," she snapped and took a long swig from her beer bottle.

"Baby, I need a drink. Bruh, I'm in serious pain," I complained sharply. "Baby get me some marijuana. You feel me?"

"Don't worry, sir! I'll take care of your pain and I'll bring you some food," she said firmly as she wheeled me down the hall.

"Where are we going?" I asked sharply, looking around.

"We're going to your room," she said calmly, guzzled the rest of her beer, and threw the bottle on the floor.

"Baby, bring me back some dope and whiskey," I said sharply.

The lady left me in room 309. There had been an old black woman moaning loudly.

"I can't believe I got to hear this broad," I said bluntly, shaking my head greenly.

"I'll be back," she said cheerfully.

She came back with medicine. She injected the medicine in my arm. A little dour Chinese woman came and left a tray of food. The crap smelled dreadful. The chicken soup, if you can call it that, had been blackish-purple. The apple pie seemed yucky too.

Three hours later on Miss Marisa Twohy came in. She had been an old girl friend. She had been likely to take me to the air-races. Her breath smelled of whiskey, barf and marijuana. She brought a bag of ribs, with a lot of sauce. Along with huge bag of greasy fries and two forty-ounce bottles of Colt 45.

"Boy, am I glad to see you, girl," I said sharply with good cheer.

"How are you feeling, bro-bro?" she asked strongly.

"Thanks to you I've come back to life. Come on. Let's get are eat-on girl!" I said sharply with a laugh.

Dog, I ripped into the ribs just like some wild animal, foaming at the mouth. Dude, I jammed a handful of fries in my mouth almost choking. I washed everything with beer.

"I thought you'd be starving," she stated strongly, standing next to my bed.

"Man, you know how I feel about this hospital stuff. I'd rather eat your turds," I said bluntly and took a long swig of beer.

"Well, did he come?" she asked strongly and she took a long swig from her beer.

"Mr. Pryce?" I said, sucking on a rib bone.

"Yeah, him," she said strongly and took an even longer guzzle of beer.

"Hello no! The frog-breath never showed," I said sharply with regret.

"Dude, I thought he had been the very best," she said dryly.

"He is. He's the coolest dude on the planet. He races planes hella tight like Marvin Gaye sings. He's great looking. He's amusing. He helps sickly kids. He makes love to the hottest babes," I stated strongly with a laugh and took a long guzzlc from my beer.

Once I finished everything Marisa put the stuff in the trash. Next, she climbed up on top of me. She kissed me. She jammed her tongue down my throat. Her breath smelled just like whiskey, barf, heavy-on-the-onions with cow breath. We made love madly. The bed squeaked like crazy. She screamed. I moaned.

Ten minutes later on, I cried out Lord-Jesus and it was over. She climbed off. We had been panting for a while.

"You were great, girl! I got my lovemaking for the day," I said strongly with a laugh. "And my hella good buzz."

"Bruh, I desire a dude that can truly satisfy me," she stated boldly with a frown.

"You don't mean that, baby," I said strongly.

"Oh, but I do," she said clearly.

"Slime you, lady! Then bounce out this joint," I said savagely.

"Baby, I was only kidding," she said strongly, grinning.

I told Marisa about the surgery, leading to the poophead Dr. Griesel neglecting me. She had been prepared to file suit against the darn hospital.

Next, the marvelous Dr. Griesel came in, smoking a massive joint.

"Where were you, jerk? Were you in the bathroom snorting coke again, with that ugly woman?" I asked hotly with an evil ghetto tone.

"No! I forgot you because I was eating girls. This sixteen year old blond little girl made me so hot," he said firmly with sadness on his face.

"Damn that little child! You're lucky dog! I had been planning to sue this damn ghetto hospital. Or have all of you folks check out to the graveyard," I stated sardonically.

"The surgery had been a success. Your monstrous tumor is gone. Gone permanently," he explained strongly, changing my IV bottle.

"Boo-boo, I hate this stuff, bruh," I stated moodily.

"This stuff can make you better," he stated sharply.

"Can I go, dog? Man, I got to see the air racer," I stated firmly, trying to get up.

"No. You can't leave! Dude, you need to remain a little longer. Bruh, you'll need rest. I don't want you going to that air race," he explained firmly, giving the black woman something to calm her down.

"Ok! Dude, I'm not going to the air-race," I said calmly.

"I'm sorry," he said firmly with regret as he guzzled some Budweiser.

"It's okay. I'll go next time the air-races are in town," I said calmly.

"Fine," he said.

"So I'm not going to die?" I asked clearly.

"Of course not my brother. Homey, you'll live forever just get some chemotherapy and radiation treatment. Man, I'll put you on chlorambucil (Leukeran), and cytoxan. You will be all right," he said strongly.

"That horrible thing isn't coming back!" I snapped.

"No...As long as you take your medicine," he said firmly.

"Yo, G. I need some marijuana!" I asked sharply.

"I'll see if I can get you some, dude," he said strongly. "I'm sure it will be easy for medical reasons."

"Listen...poop-breath bum! Don't ever leave me in that operating room again or I'll kick your butt-in," I stated hotly.

"All right!" he snapped. "I really sorry."

As soon as the physician left, I asked Marisa to get my clothes. I battled to get dressed. Dog, I strolled out with Marisa on my arm and was still very weak. The dumb doctor didn't catch me. She'd a face just like a boxer and bad skin. But compelling. I still adored her.

Dog, I turned up at Johnathan Pryce's fancy garage. An old woman dressed just like a housewife had been hanging around. His giant-ass F-16 parked close by. There were clearly no young girls. It was just this old woman. What happened to the pretty girls?

Once I stepped inside a black man with a badly scared up face was sitting in a chair. He appeared to be masturbating with a Playboy magazine in his lap. A beautiful coffee skinned young girl had been on the cover. There had been a lot of empty Olde English beer cans scattered about on the floor. Two empty Canadian Mist bottles on the chair.

"Hello, I'm Dijon Lamont," I said strongly with a smile.

"What the hell?" He stated spitefully with an evil gaze. He chucked the magazine. After that stood and pulled up his pants. "What are you

some kind of pervert, punk?" he stated
sardonically.

"Yo, old-bruh, I'm looking for Mr.
Johnathan Pryce," I stated firmly.

"You're looking at him, dude," he said hotly,
looking over piercingly.

His breath smelled like boiled rotten
lunchmeat and whiskey and he appeared to be
hella tore up.

"You look like a cracked-out smoking dude
trying to steal Mr. Pryce's plane," I said self-
righteously, regarding with cold speculation.

The cat was six feet tall and temperamental
bum.

"What do you want, dog?" he snapped loudly.

"Bruh, I'm dying of cancer. You were supposed to come see me. You're my hero. What went down?" I said bluntly.

"Oh, I thought you were a kid. Dog, I went to the Children's Hospital. You dig?" he said calmly.

"No, old-gee. I was at Brook Bear Hospital," I said firmly.

"Well, you told me. Let's have a drink. You do drink?" he asked calmly.

"Always!" I stated strongly with a laugh.

We sat for hours talking, hella lying, farting, burping and drinking Wild Turkey and laughing. He put on some music---Ice Cube. He told me interesting stories about his outstanding air-racing career. He had an awful scare on his forehead. He had some blue stuff in his left eye. He wasn't a tall man or a short one.

"Why are you drinking and taking pills?" I asked firmly with frown.

"I'm in pain, dawg. I'm all messed up. Boo, I've been in several crashes. Will you fly with me, brother?" he asked sharply.

"Now?" I asked strongly, blinking excessively.

"Yeh...now, dog!" Mr. Pryce said fiercely with a laugh.

"Oh, Lawd," I stated strongly with my face grown ashen.

"Get your booty in the damn plane," Pryce stated strongly.

We wandered over to his F-16. He strolled with a limp. His horrid face had been twisted in pain as he moved slowly. He opened the giant bubble looking top. Dude, I climbed in and fastened my seatbelt. It took him along time to get in. All the bright colored buttons and switches baffled me. But then again, I'm not the pilot.

Pryce pushes a few switches and shifted knobs. It was an easy task to him. All routine. The big beast blades began to move, engine cranked over. The force made the plane shake and quivered.

We were off, collecting speed as we went down a narrow runway. Abruptly the plane plunged upward into the grey sky. The impact drew me back into the seat like a suction cup. At five hundred miles per hour, it didn't take very long to reach 4,200ft. My head had been glued to the headrest the force wouldn't allow me to move an inch. Dog, I felt my skin sliding off my face, along with tears. My heart was pounding like a Speed freak.

Then this thing went down. Dog, I felt just like I was riding on a damn sub missile. Once we came lower around the downtown area at 765 mph, he pulled the lever down, and merely missed the top of the Harrah's casino. I pissed and pooped my pants.

We did somersaults and extravagant aerobatics on the way back at 506 mph. We flew through traffic and in between giant casino buildings---very narrow passages. We flew through the Reno casino without touching anything or persons. Next Pryce ejected himself from the plane.

I'm sure this cat left the plane in autopilot. The plane dipped down swiftly past Pryce's body as he sunk rapidly downward through the sky. The plane quickly leveled itself back so he could drop back inside the planes cockpit easily. We flew back up before crashing into the top of the Circus-Circus casino. We flew through small rings of fire. That drunken pilot wasn't fazed at all. The whole experience had been off-the-chisel. We landed in Pryce's empty swimming pool.

When I climbed out of the super-cool bird, I threw-up. Mr. Pryce fell out of the cockpit, landing on his back and his stoned butt was out cold. A jaunty man, wearing greasy coveralls, picked him up over his shoulders and carried him inside the garage.

It had been the coolest stuff I ever encountered. I must have been crazy as hell to go up in an airplane with a man full of whiskey and pills. Yet for some reason he'd total control of this beast. Just like a poet over an audience at good poetry reading.

Dog, I sat with a bunch of sickly folks for a boring hour, observing medicine drip from an IV bottle with nasty junk into my arm. Everybody had been trying to have a sense of humor about this stuff. After that, I felt sick. But it didn't matter. Dude, I had to eat. I needed to keep my strength up. I ate Manhattan clam chowder. Two hours later, I threw-up.

Boo, I don't know where I got the strength, yet I managed to give Marisa one of my wild lovemaking romps. We drank Wild Turkey for many hours. After that, we staggered over to the race. It had been held outside of Stead, NV. It had been nippy. Marisa dressed in red blouse and pink shorts. I wore a red shirt and baggy blue jeans that kept falling off my booty.

Once we got there the race already begun, Marisa began having a hotdog packed with catsup and onions. She washed it down with a bottle of Jack Daniels she brought. I threw up again. There was Calvert's vivid pink Mustang P-51, thrusting through the blue sky. The engine roared loudly. Calvert had been gay. He had been the only openly gay man in the race. He was quick and clever too. But he had trouble with Pryce.

"The gay dude is closing in on Pryce," Marisa said strongly with a worried gaze.

"No, never! That hella dope smoking pilot is too fast. That homeboy's F-16 is too fast. P-51's are too slow," I said strongly with a weak laugh.

"The noises of the engines are really loud," she lamented strongly and she took a long swig of whiskey.

"Cover your ears, girl," I stated firmly.

"We better not stay very long. Bruh, you seem too weak. You have to go lay down," she said sharply, passing me the bottle.

"No! Boo, I'll be all right. Stop fussing," I said bluntly and took a long-ass guzzle from the bottle.

There were many planes.

"They're more planes this year," she said strongly, finishing her hotdog.

"Bruh, I like the Blackhawk, SR-71 Blackbird, and F-16 Falcon, which hella rocks. Let us not forget those cool F-22's and MIG-25's," I said strongly with a laugh.

"Look at that X-15," she said sharply, beaming.

"That thing---it's too fast. Boo-boo, you can't race those planes here," I said and took another long swig of whiskey.

"Why Dijon?" she asked firmly, lighting a joint.

"Those baby's move quicker than 10,000 mph," I stated strongly and took a long swig of the whiskey.

They managed all sorts of tricks. Yet Pryce performed probably the most risky. That's exactly what made the race hella awesome. That frog-brain homeboy was crazy. That bum Pryce flew at us at 590 mph, audience disperse just like damn roaches when a light is switched on. At the right time, he flew back up, clipping several tree limbs as he did. No one had his guts and balls.

After the race, we ran into Mr. Pryce, clutching onto a big gold trophy of an F-15 aircraft. He had been staggering up to us. I could smell the booze while he was 4,000 ft. in the sky.

"Are you drunk, homey?" I asked firmly with a laugh.

"Dog, I better be," he said strongly with a laugh.

"Dude, why?" I asked seriously and took another longer swig of whiskey.

"I told you, kid. It stops the pain. The agony is in my bum leg," he said sharply.

"How did you injure your leg, sir?" she asked strongly and took a long drag of weed.

"I've been in a few accidents, baby-girl. My leg has already been shattered in four places. I lost my eye. My nose is certainly broken up. I lost two of my fingers and part of my left foot.

"I can't believe the officials let you do this stuff, bruh," I said strongly, giving a startled gasp.

"They all adore me, kid. You feel me?" he stated boastfully.

His stinky racing uniform had been loaded with major sponsors and grease.

"They are crazy," she said harshly, looking over piercingly.

"Who is this lovely creature?" he asked sharply, gazing at candidly.

"My good friend Marisa Twoby," I said firmly with a smile.

Pryce grabbed her hand. As he attempted to kiss it, she snatched her hand away.

"Bruh, I love her. Isn't Miss Twoby a party-goer?"

"She gets her party-on," I added strongly with a laugh and pasted the whiskey to her.

"I thought you were dead already, brother. You dig?" he said strongly with a laugh.

"My cancer is in remission, bruh," I said firmly.

"Well, kid. I have to cut. Won't you catch my upcoming race, young blood?" he said strongly with good cheer.

"Old-dog, I certainly can. You're my one and only homeboy," I said sharply with a smile.

"Good!" he said cheerfully.

"See you around bum-breath!" I said strongly with a laugh and walked off.

Pryce limped back into his garage, wincing. He nearly dropped his trophies. I should've helped him but I didn't.

"Look at this awful dude," Marisa said sourly and took a long swig of whiskey. "He's a fool-bum!"

"I see," I said clearly.

"How could you idolize this bird-brain?" she asked caustically and took an even longer guzzle of whiskey.

"I don't know bruh. I just thought the homeboy was hella cool. Dog, I don't know how this artistic bird-brain can fly a plane that way," I said strongly.

"Look there's seven unsightly folks standing in line, for an autograph," she explained dryly.

"Well...it's early yet," I said.

"Let's go. I want to get hella tore up! I hate this maggot-man. I don't care how good he flies. He's sardonic. Slime him, bruh!" she said strongly and continued to sip on the bottle.

"Bruh, I do too. Yet I'm planning to see this cat tomorrow," I stated firmly.

Dog, I took Marisa home. I stopped by Edobor's Liquor store, snapped up a six-pack, and traveled to my shabby room. Dude, I drank Cobra and had taken a bunch of horrible pills.

And sprayed a half of can of bug spray on my tongue to farther my high. I threw-up. I'd runny stools. My head and tummy hurt. Cancer is bad, bro-bro. Now I see how that pilot dude feels.

On the day of Pryce last race, I had been there. And thus had been a great deal of folks too. Marisa refused to come even when I agreed to buy that woman a bottle of Jack Daniels. I had been fragile and so I couldn't stand very long. You feel me? This brawny dude, with sophomoric sense of humor, hoisted me onto his shoulders. What I could see was a number of first-rate planes, burning-up the sky. The roaring engines shook the blue sky. I needed to cover my ears sometimes. Pryce had been in the lead from the start.

Abruptly Pryce's F-16 Falcon backed off from the rest of the planes arched downward, at 676-mph. right into a mountain. Next, an ear-piercing explosion followed. Red, and orange flames and black smoke rose from the mountain. Many viewers cringed, and their faces became glum. There had been screaming and crying.

The brawny artless dude began to run through the crowd with me still on his shoulders. I practically fell over.

"Dude, I must save Mr. Pryce," he yelled sharply.

"No! Stop. You crazy idiot! I'll fall," I stated bluntly.

He lifted me off, and dropped me down in the crowd of saddened Pryce fans. Dude, I was nearly torn to pieces.

"Slime you, dog! You retard," I shouted sharply to him.

The dimwit pushed through the crowd. Dude, I stood by a telephone pole. Bruh, I heard the noise of sirens at a distance. I suspected this stuff was going to happen. That blockhead. Why fly hella stoned out of your head? You're too messed up, bruh. What happened to my idol? Why did I worship this worthless homey?

Several months later, I sat in the cancer office with seven other sick folks. John experienced prostate cancer. Mary had breast cancer. Peter had bone cancer.

The cops had decided that Air-Racer Johnathan Pryce's death had been an accident. An excessive amount of booze and medication impaired his judgment whilst air racing.

Just a couple of weeks ago the cops found out new evidence. The coroner did a double check on Pryce's heavy burned body. They discovered some cyanide in an apple pie that he may have eaten earlier. Bridget Huttman baked an apple pie for him. It had been that old bitty I noticed hanging around his garage. Mr. Pryce always received lot of Olde English beer, marijuana and gifts from his fans and her too.

The main reason Mrs. Huttman murdered Mr. Pryce was that her grandson, Gene Aleman, went along to jail for robbing a 7-11. Whilst in jail a gay man with AIDS raped him in the bathroom. Aleman died a couple of years ago.

Yet the young man, Aleman, didn't do it. Pryce had been heading for a 7-11 for a bottle of whiskey. Once Aleman went along to the store to purchase soda pop, he noticed the store clerk on the floor, bleeding. He listened to the siren and saw Mr. Pryce wandering towards the store. So he ran down the street. Pryce mistook Aleman for the robber and murderer of the store clerk.

The real killer was Terrence Berkowitz. He is now in jail serving life.

Dog, it's funny the way we idolize folks and believe they are able to do no wrong, just like angles. We presume they're perfect, yet they're not. We look up to them. We count on them to set examples for all of us...especially our children. Yet they're just like the rest of us. They're total screw-ups.

The Scandalous Birds

The Oakland Airport suffered a significant problem---gulls, pelicans, ducks and cormorants and all kinds of birds. They organized a conference at the end of the runway. On a busy Saturday, an Oakland Air flight had taken off at the end of the runway, killing a number of birds-once they got spooked, and flew up in the planes powerful blades.

Subsequently on Sunday, an Oakland Air plane veered off the end of the runway, once the aviator stumbled on a hundred birds meeting there, likely to take control the city of Oakland. There were several injuries occurred.

The airport supervisor, Mr. Steve Barraco, had been getting his ass beaten down by Fish & Gaming, animal activists and wildlife supporters. There were clearly 5,500 birds slaughtered in a month. As a result, he hired this kind of bird-brain private investigator, Mr. Gene Flax, a brawny-looking dude, bovine, and a fat-face bum, with a tobacco-roughened voice. He smelled just like hog sewage and sweated poodles of water everywhere. He dressed in Salvation Army clothes. Yet he'd good results. He did time for having Marijuana and fooling around with fifteen-year-old black girls. Flax gave Mr. Barraco plenty of trouble about the job. Once he offered him a ton of money, he gave in.

Well, Flax's first day on the job was successful. At the least 100 birds relaxed on the end of the runway. Flax took a lengthy white hose. After that, he switched the water full-blast on those birds.

"This will certainly take care of you bums," Flax muttered harshly as he pulled on a joint dangling from his mouth.

The birds and pigeons swiftly rose from the asphalt and travelled into the skies. Dude, it had taken around five minute for them all to go. Barraco came out to deal with Flax wearing a blue suit.

"Dude, are you crazy, dog?" Mr. Barraco asked stubbornly with an ugly gaze.

"Bruh, I got rid of those frog-poops, didn't I?" Mr. Flax said hotly. "That's what you pay me for gee!"

"Dude, I might have done that, frog-brain," Mr. Barraco snapped, turning a cold eye on.

"Yo, black man. You can't be a coward homeboy with these Scandalous birds. They'll hella clown you homeboy," Flax stated sharply and took a long drag of weed as he replaced the hose.

"Fishing and Gaming, wildlife and animal lovers are likely to bust a clip in my booty once they see this. I can't believe I hired this dumb fish-turd," Mr. Barraco stated spitefully.

"Slime these folks, dude. Relax a bit. Get your butt back in the office and quit tripping. Allow me to do my job, son," he snapped and went.

The following several planes came down the runway with relieve.

Just incase Flax hung around in a 2002 blue Dodge truck. He had been parked where he could see the runway. He sat smoking marijuana and drinking beer all day, watching planes lift off. Folks left the airport, transporting luggage, going in, coming out, and getting in taxis, and shuttle buses, stepping out of them. You know the typical boring stuff. The gulls didn't come back. Therefore, he left.

Later on that night, the pig-face dude had been high as a kite. He drove down to 62nd street, East of Oakland, not really an enjoyable location, yet it had been his sorta scene. A long-legged black chick, with coco butter skin, was standing on the corner. She dressed in a red silk dress covered with a lengthy leather coat. She must have been fourteen or so.

Indisputably, she was ready for some lovemaking. Mr. Flax got out of his truck, wandered over to this lady. He hoped to introduce himself.

In a short time, Flax had been shoving her up against the back corner of McDonalds, which had been closed. The fat made love to her wildly, smacking her around. Then it was over quick. Once he pulled up his extra large jeans as he was panting, he had been hit hard on the back of the head. He turned around. What looked like a traitorous black man struck him on the forehead. The black chick got frightened and bailed. The black man backed away. Flax came forward, hurling a right. The black man dodged it. And the black man came back with a large rock, bashing the big-dog in the head and kicked him in the nuts. Flax winced as he fell over onto the ground.

Whilst Flax had been on the ground, the black man kicked him many times. Next, he had taken the man's keys and all his money. He then had taken off in his truck.

Mr. Barraco phoned Flax. He had been annoyed due to the fact three hundred birds made their home back on the runway.

"All right! Just calm down, cuz," Flax stated strongly in the phone.

"Calm down! Those birds attacked three homeless people and killed them," Barraco claimed firmly.

"Ok. Don't trip! Dog, I'll be right over," he explained bitterly, slamming the phone down.

When Flax turned up, limping up to the runway. He brought a Chinese girl, Joyce Ho. She had been tiny, lovely, assertive, and young. Flax eyes had been slits. His face had been badly bruised and puffy, like some loser boxer. They were transporting a few scrapers. Mr. Barraco had been on the runway with a withering stare.

"Who is this?" Mr. Barraco inquired testily.

"Miss Ho is my charming assistant, dude," Flax explained strongly and took a long drag of weed.

"What happened to you?" Mr. Barraco asked hotly.

"My dumb butt fell down a flight of stairs, yet I'm cool," Flax stated strongly with a weak smile.

"Man, I assumed she kicked your butt, bro-bro," Barraco stated firmly with a laugh.

"No, never! Dude," Flax stated strongly.

"And you're past due," Mr. Barraco said boldly.

"Dude, shut up! The sole reason I put up with your hating ass, due to the fact I don't want those bum-butts to take my house. Or else, I wouldn't have considered this fake case. I favor divorce and missing person cases. Dude, I'm a private investigator not really a Fish & Gaming and wildlife smuck," Flax explained strongly, looking over piercingly and took a long drag of weed.

"What are you doing with that thing?" Barraco inquired sharply studying acutely.

"We're cleaning up all the bird dukey," Mr. Flax said calmly, blowing smoke in his face.

"Well, could there be anything I can do?" Barraco inquired calmly.

"Yeah, shag your butt back into the office and allow me to do my job, jerk-off," Flax stated strongly, finishing his joint.

With some substantial effort, Flax got three hundred furious birds to go away. He scraped several pounds of bird poop from the runway as

Miss Ho hosed everything down. It had taken them all night.

The following day these birds had been back. There must have been a couple hundred thousand this time around. Mr. Flax had thrown out a ton of poison bird feed on the other side of the runway. Mr. Flax sat in his 2001 white Buick, drinking on a forty ounce Olde English bottle of beer, whilst Miss Ho kissed his face. He observed the scandalous birds. Those hella gangsters huddled on the runway, plotting to kill us all. Their thoughts are justified. All things considered we've hunted them, killing a lot of those poop-brains, he said to himself. We've cooked and eaten them. Every since they've existed. After hours of sitting there, the birds made no move towards the bird feed.

"Those things happen to be wiser than I thought," Flax said strongly and took a long swig of beer.

"What do we do now, honey?" she inquired strongly with worry shown on her face.

"Let's get high, boo-boo," he stated sharply, lighting a cigar size joint.

He drank four more big Olde English bottles of beer and staggered about the area collecting rocks with Miss Ho. Next, they started hurling them at the birds. The birds tweeted loudly as some of them flew off. They kept throwing rock until the birds dispersed away.

"That will teach those scandalous bums, baby-girl," Flax stated strongly with a big laugh and lit another big joint.

"Yeah. Take a look at them fly off like cowards," Miss Ho added sharply with good cheer.

Mr. Flax drove from down East Oakland. He identified the black man from the other night. Flax pulled up beside him.

"Hey, player! Remember me?" he said strongly with a laugh.

The black man looked at him. After that Flax produced a Browning BDA .38 Super Auto. He opened fire as the man attempted to run off. The bullets ripped through the man's back as he flung forward, landing on his stomach.

Next, the fat man fired several more shots into the body as he sped off just incase the dude was still alive. He was certain the man was dead now.

He stopped at McDonald's and sat in a parking lot, eating one of ten-quarter pounders with seven orders of fries. He flushed everything down with two forty-ounce bottles of Mickey's. After dinner, he sat in his car smoking a massive joint and farting.

Back at the Oakland Airport, those scandalous birds returned. Three thousand. Mr.

Flax had taken out a gun and began shooting into the large gang of birds.

"Sorry, I had to go gangsta. However, you homeboy's can't be holding assembly on the runway no more. You feel me? Didn't you realize planes need to come through here?" flax snapped and took a long swig of Midnight Moon.

The birds tweeted loudly saying, "Bug off" in bird language. The noise had been deafening. Mr. Flax strolled back holding his ears.

"You bird-brains...you frog-turds cost the airport a ton of money. It's nothing personal. I'm planning to take you out of the game," he stated bluntly.

The birds seem to understand what he was saying and a number of the birds flew up into his face. He batted them away with his arms. Yet their razor-sharp claws and beaks cut up his face pretty good. There seemed to be a lot of blood. Thankfully, he wore glasses, which safeguarded his eyes from those evil bums.

"Screw you! You vicious dog-breaths," Flax screamed venomously, firing shots at the birds wildly not realizing anyone of those bullets could hit somebody.

Mr. Flax slaughtered many of those wild birds but many more came back even madder.

The birds got very angry with him. They charged at him, viciously pecking his head, face and body. Blood emerged from his wounds. He ran for the airport, dropping the gun. The birds had completely covered him, digging their beaks into his flesh. There was a lot of blood. He fell and got back up. The birds attacked taxi drivers, shuttle-bus folks, tourist and maintenance. Flax ran into the airport Thousands of birds started in there. Those crazed birds attacked everybody. Folks screamed. They ran into each other, trying to get away. Folks were being trampled to death and kids too. It had been a horrible scene.

Mr. Flax got the majority of the birds off him. He snapped up these two screaming kids being eaten on by black birds. The kid's faces had chunks of flesh missing. The kids seemed to be in shock. They ran into the restroom. This bull had been just like a darn movie.

"Why do birds hate people?" the boy inquired strongly, gulping spastically.

"I don't know, son. I believe we'd this coming," Flax clarified sharply, shaking his head greenly.

Many folks came in to the restroom. It was beginning to seem like a sardine can. They had been weeping hysterically and bloody too.

Two or three hours later on the loud tweeting stopped and birds were leaving the airport.

Flax came forth from the bathroom. There was clearly several bodies spread about the airport. The birds had been gone. Plenty of dead folks and their children had their eyes gorged out. There had been folks with their kids nursing serious cuts and bruises sobbing over loved ones. Yet many folks were in shock and sustained cuts and bruises. The paramedics had been patching up hysterical folks. The coroner had been removing bodies.

Mr. Barraco limped up to Flax. His face had been bloody. His suit had been torn. He was cynical and deranged. He punched Flax into the face with a hard right, forcing a tooth to fall out and Flax spit blood on him.

"You slimeball! You started all this stuff. Why did you shoot at them?" Barraco asked bluntly.

Flax was in worst shape.

"What did you want me to do-kiss the punks?" Flax said hotly.

"I just don't like the way you handled this," Barraco stated testily.

"Those evil birds are gone, aren't they?" Flax snapped.

"Look at all these dead folks. We'll be slapped with plenty of lawsuits. You feel me?" Mr. Barraco said caustically with a scorching look.

"You retained me to get rid of the birds, homeboy. And I did just that," Flax said strongly, turning around and wandered away.

"Slime you! You are going to pay for this. You fat manic," Barraco yelled sharply.

"This is your mess homeboy. And the damn Fish & Game and animal lovers too. You ought to have left those wild birds alone to begin with," Flax snapped. "Also you have to send the medic team in the restroom. There are a handful of injured folks in there, too."

"Stop that crazy bum. I want the cops to arrest that frog-brain! You feel me?" Mr. Barraco said ruthlessly.

The victim's family members filed lawsuits against the airport---suit that are still pending. The birds never came back to the runway. Mr. Barraco had been fired for the way he handled everything. Mr. Flax had been arrested for soliciting prostitution from three Chinese girls under fifteen. Once the PI got out, he went into the limo service business.

THE END

About The Author

I live in the Bay Area and have lived in Nevada. I worked as a busboy while writing stuff about Russia. From there I studied writing at a community collage but because of alcohol problems, I missed a lot of classes. I wrote a potent small collection of stories called Darryl's Crime Files, which is in paperback at Amazon. My goal is to get a million readers because reading is very important and so many people can't read. I want to end this especially in poor neighborhoods. If you have a copy of this book, I want to thank you your support.

www.ingramcontent.com/pod-product-compliance
Lightning Source LLC
Chambersburg PA
CBHW020518290526
45786CB00002B/666